PAY OFF

your

MORTGAGE

PAY DOWN YOUR
BIGGEST DEBT FAST

THE KEY TO
FINANCIAL FREEDOM

DANIEL RONDBERG

Printed in the United States of America

ISBN: 978-1-7349613-1-7

Published by Cass&Spence Publishing LLC, Arizona

Disclaimer

This publication is designed to provide accurate and authoritative information with regard to the subject matter covered. It is sold with the understanding that the publisher is not engaged in rendering legal, accounting, or other professional advice. If legal advice or other expert assistance is required, the services of a competent professional should be sought.

The author wishes to acknowledge the respective sources for use of graphs, charts, and other data in this book, and it is the author's intent to portray that data accurately rather than through representations.

This book may contain technical or other errors. Daniel Rondberg and The Retirement Research Foundation do not guarantee its accuracy, completeness, or suitability. In no event shall Daniel Rondberg or The Retirement Research Foundation be liable for any special, indirect, or consequential damages relating to this material for any use of this material or for any referenced website and courses, or the application of any idea or strategy in this book.

The information contained in this book is provided by Daniel Rondberg and The Retirement Research Foundation, and it is offered for educational and informational purposes only. Daniel Rondberg is a licensed insurance agent. He suggests that you consult with a qualified legal or tax-planning professional with regard to your personal circumstances. Nothing in this book should be interpreted or construed as legal, regulatory, insurance, tax, or financial planning advice or as an offer to perform services related to any of these fields in any respect.

The content of this book contains general information and may not reflect current legal, tax, insurance, or regulatory developments and information, and it is not guaranteed to be correct, complete, or current. Daniel Rondberg and The Retirement Research Foundation makes no warranty, expressed or implied, as to the accuracy or reliability of this information or the information contained in any referenced website or course.

Readers of this book should not act or refrain from acting on the basis of any information included herein without seeking appropriate legal or other relevant advice related to the particular facts and circumstances at issue from an attorney or other advisor duly and properly licensed in the recipient's state of residence. Daniel Rondberg and The Retirement Research Foundation expressly disclaim all liability with respect to actions taken or not taken by the reader based on any or all of the information or other contents within this book or provided by Daniel directly. Any information sent to Daniel Rondberg or The Retirement Research Foundation via Internet, e-mail, or through any referenced website is not secure and is done so on a non-confidential basis.

Should the reader of this book seek a referral to any service provider, the person to whom such referral is made is solely responsible for assessing the knowledge, skill, or capabilities of such provider, and neither the author, presenter, nor The Retirement Research Foundation is responsible for the quality, integrity, performance, or any other aspect of any services ultimately provided by such provider or any damages, consequential or incidental, arising from the use of such provider. Any opinions expressed in the book are mine alone and mine based on the information publicly available to me in my interpretation of that information.

Dedication

To my girls. This is my first step in becoming an author so I can spend more time with you every day.

Table of Contents

Preface

Have you ever read a book to learn how to do something? Did you wish the author would get right to the point so that you could obtain the knowledge you need and start using it right away? Was the book filled with fluff that tried to prove to you how smart the author was? Were you frustrated sifting through unnecessary pages? Have you ever finished reading a book and realized the information you actually wanted to know could have been explained in 50 pages instead of 200 pages? Me, too!

So, enter my new career as an Amazon Short Reads author. I will be writing a series of short books that will, in under 100 pages, deliver the best strategies I have picked up in my career as a retirement consultant. My day job is to help my clients create security and certainty in their retirement. I love what I do – so much so that I pride myself on providing as much value as I can to each client that sits down with me. My passion is sharing the nonconventional, most valuable, and meaningful information that can make a tremendous difference in others' lives.

In 2018, I realized that I could only help so many people per year through one-on-one meetings. So, I accepted an offer to travel the country, bringing my message to the financial community. I was hired to speak to and train insurance agents, financial advisors, CPAs, and attorneys on strategies for retirees to maximize the Tax Cuts and Jobs Act (The Tax Reform). My theory was that if I spoke to 100 financial professionals at once, and they each had 100 clients, I was significantly expanding my impact and potentially helping many more people.

After my lectures, attendees would often tell me that I should consider writing a book. So, I wrote my first book, "No Stone Left Unturned: How to Cash in on this Hidden Treasure in the Tax Code (That Can Save You Hundreds of Thousands in Retirement)." I figured by moonlighting as an author, I could use Amazon's platform to really expand the reach of my message and help even more people. The book has become an International Best Seller in several categories.

However, it took me more than 2,000 hours to write that book. I considered it my life's work, so I approached writing it as if it were my masterpiece. It would be my final contribution to the retirement education space, and I wanted it to be perfect. I obsessed over it. I instructed my wife to physically smack me upside my head if I ever uttered the words, "I'm going to write another book." I told her to remind me of when I stayed up all night, writing over 3,000 words only to accidentally delete it all 30 minutes before it was time for me to get ready for work.

You might be wondering how and why I wrote this book. Well, I learned many things while writing my first book. Most importantly, I could deliver the most critical part of my message more effectively in fewer words. I realized I don't need to impress you. I don't care if you like my cover. I think you might even, dare I say it…no it's unthinkable, forgive a typo??? I wouldn't forgive myself, but seriously, if I could spend less than $15 and read fewer than 50 pages to learn a secret in finance that could allow me to accomplish my goal faster, I'd take that over a fancy bibliography every day of the week.

So, here I am. "No Stone Left Unturned" is my flagship book that I will be expanding into this short-read series. I truly believe in leaving no stone unturned when clients trust me to help them. It's how I want to be treated. I want anyone working for me to be willing to exhaust every possible option and approach education with the tenacity to find all possible solutions—conventional and nonconventional. When I refer to a solution as "nonconventional," please do infer it is less legitimate.

What I mean by nonconventional is we are taught virtually nothing about finance in school, but what does society teach us?

- ✓ Spend 20 years on an education, work for 40 years, and then retire for 20 years.
- ✓ Go to college. Student loans are OK because they are a down payment for your future career.
- ✓ Buy a home with a 30-year mortgage because that's safe and a great investment.
- ✓ Contribute to your 401(k), maximize your contributions and make sure you get the company match, diversify, buy and hold, close your eyes.
- ✓ Wake up 40 years later a millionaire, drop your life insurance because your home is paid off.
- ✓ Shop the lowest rates and refinance to lower your payment.
- ✓ And on and on and on.

But everyone's situation is different. Wherever you are in life, it is essential to align this education with your goal. If it does not align with your goal, that is equally as important and useful in this process. People often set arbitrary goals because they don't know what they really want. So, they don't achieve the goal because when things got tough, there was no desire to go through that pain threshold to stick with it.

It was society's goal. "Have one million dollars to retire with at age 65." Really? Says who? You don't know what I want, but yet you're willing to tell me what I should do? This is a much deeper cultural issue. We have a problem as a society with *fear of missing out* or (FOMO) and getting our financial education from people selling products to us.

Enter the mortgage broker and the 30-year fixed mortgage. Let me be clear – I did not write this book to wage war on the mortgage business – I am a licensed loan originator. I wrote this book to expose the problem and show you how to fix it. You have a mortgage, and you have a goal of paying it off much quicker than in 30 years.

First I will help you identify your goal and understand why it's important to you, and then I will show you how to accelerate the mortgage payoff to five years or less.

Introduction

Having a goal is great if it gets you what YOU truly desire more than anything, and if you map your actions to accomplish it. Don't spend your life chasing arbitrary goals for someone else's approval. For example, saying "Starting Monday, I'm going to lose ten pounds" because in two months, you're going on a family beach vacation and you're afraid what people will think when they see you in a swimsuit. Often, we buy homes that don't fit our lifestyle to impress people who never come over. Crazy, right? Most Americans spend roughly 70% of their time in less than 900 square feet of their home.

The first home I purchased was impressive for a 25-year-old, but my wife and I found that we weren't using most of it. We had a beautiful dining room that we used twice for Thanksgiving dinners. We had an acre of land but rarely went outside. We seldom went upstairs, yet we paid the principal, interest, taxes, insurance, and maintenance on nearly 2,000 square feet of "look at me" house. It was someone else's goal, not ours.

Don't stop reading now. I am not encouraging you to downsize. I am encouraging you to have a real conversation, either with yourself (or with your partner). Be as honest as possible and ask yourself what it is about your current living situation that you no longer desire.

I am not a minimalist, but it is so important to get in touch with what YOU truly desire more than anything. For most Americans, housing is their largest monthly expense. And while being at home may bring you joy, paying the bank usually doesn't.

So, let's talk *Free and Clear* for a second. It is empowering. It can certainly lessen the need to produce a high amount of after-tax money, which will grant easier access to retirement. In the space below, write down why you want to own your home free and clear. Be as honest and detailed as possible. No one will see your answer, and it will be helpful later.

House Hacking

The path to owning your home Free and Clear can be challenging. Rather than downsizing or taking on a side hustle to make extra payments, ask yourself if you didn't have to make the payment, would that serve your goal? Don't worry; I'm not going to talk about reverse mortgages. I'm talking about house hacking.

There are many ways to house hack, but the simplest and most effective method is buying a home with another living space attached. This can be a duplex, basement, mother-in-law suite, or an additional apartment or house on the property. The rent collected from this other space can cover your mortgage. You can also have roommates or offer a room(s) as Airbnb's.

Some homeowners use the equity in their homes to purchase rental properties with the goal of paying their mortgage with the profits from those rental properties.

Some people say: "Well, that's great if your single and in your early 20's. What about if you're married with two kids?"

Well, I'm going to show you how to pay off your mortgage in five years or less. (This book is not about house hacking, but to help you achieve your goal, I thought it was at least important to mention.) So, how do you do it? Let's dive in!

I promised you a concise message, so here you go. If you refinance your 30-year fixed mortgage to a first lien home equity line of credit, you can turn the amortization tables to your favor and accelerate the balance down to zero in five years. If you want the formula and strategy, skip ahead to "The Solution: Home Equity Lines of Credit." Find the answer, then go back to "The Problem: Mortgages" for supporting evidence that this method is legitimate and effective.

BONUS

Let's say you are reading this and you're not the up and comer. You are on the doorstep of or are in retirement now, and you have a mortgage. There is a product called a Home Equity Conversion Mortgage (HECM). An HECM does fall in the reverse mortgage family, but DO NOT STOP READING. Remember what I said earlier about financial education. It should not come from people selling you products or from someone who heard something from someone else and then passed it on like a bad game of telephone, from someone who has no idea what the original message was.

The HECM will do three things:

1. Stop your principal and interest payments. You will always pay taxes and insurance, so that is a non-issue. It's a non-recourse loan, meaning you do not pay it back in monthly amortized payments. Any balance you have will still accrue interest, but you are not required to make a payment.

2. Protect the value of your home. Let me give you an example. Say your home is worth $300,000 of "equity." Your neighbor has a short sale, and all of a sudden, your home is worth $260,000. How many of you, especially those in retirement, would love to go back and capture your $40,000 that vanished? Of course, you would! You worked hard for that money. The HECM will do that.

3. Provide tax-free liquidity to equity, and the line grows every year by the interest rate. This is one example of a higher interest rate benefiting you by providing potentially more line utilization.

There are a few downsides to using this strategy.

1. Higher closing costs and rates which can be expensive and eat into your equity.
2. It's not the best option for people who may want to relocate in the next few years.
3. It's not for people who desire to leave their primary residence to their heirs.
4. You must be at least 62 to apply and there are also strict loan to value requirements.

This is a brief overview of HECMs, which are not the main subject of this book. If you want more information about HECMs, speak with your mortgage broker about these products. While I'm at it, disclaimer time!

Everyone's scenario is different and should be properly evaluated by a team of licensed advisors. No strategy in this book should be executed without the guidance of advisors. Nothing in this book should be taken as investment, tax, or advice of any kind.

Financial Freedom

This book is just another step on the path towards financial freedom for years to come. Personal finance isn't taught in schools. Most of us learn it from our parents. Their financial habits, good or bad, usually have an impact on our financial futures.

Money and finances are the leading cause of divorces in the United States. People incur tremendous stress and endure health problems from the lack of means to receive proper medical care or to eat the right foods.

Money can do many things:

- Dictate your expressions of love for your spouse, family, and friends.
- Dictate our free time.
- Make us do things we hate for years.
- Cause depression and anxiety.
- Cause us to become people that we are not.
- Cause us to cross moral agreements and break laws.
- Drive us away from people.

- Make us bitter, envious, and miserable.
- Take away from us experiencing this world to the fullest, with the one life we get.

Many of us worry 24/7 about money, and we don't even realize it.

Money can also:

- Provide freedom in our lives.
- Allow us to live like kings and queens compared to the rest of the world.
- Allow us to give back and share love and joy with people who need us.
- Provide the most amazing experiences. We can take our spouses, children, and friends around the world sampling and enjoying all of the culture and natural wonder our souls can handle.
- Provide us time to enjoy life and pursue the passions we truly want to explore.
- Provide you everything you need to live your life to the fullest.
- Build a legacy that allows your family to take control and break the cycle of poverty.
- Be an afterthought. A tool. A means to living the life you've always wanted.

So how can money make you both miserable and joyful? Why is it that one moment you feel scarcity and the next you feel abundance? Because money is 100% psychological. The older I get, the more I think that is true. People carry around fixed beliefs and have strong emotional responses to money. We are also constantly being programmed to think about money on a never-ending basis. You always seem to have enough and, somehow, it is never enough. This is because we bounce back and forth between feeling content and wanting more. My goal is to help you find strategies that reduce the burden of constantly feeling like you need to make more money and instead help you make the most with what you have.

NO STONE LEFT UNTURNED

When my wife had our first daughter, everything in my life changed. My priorities changed. My desires changed. I was obsessed with only one thing: spending as much time with my wife and daughter as I could. I had a great career, but unless I was there to work it, I had no income. It began to hurt knowing that I was trapped. I grew miserable trying to comprehend that I had to leave this little girl and the love of my life every morning and be apart from them all day. I had no choice.

I began to grasp for education. I found people and tools that promised the highest income possible. I spent countless hours and tens of thousands of dollars on every product you could think of to make or save money. I searched everywhere on the internet. It began to consume me. Every conversation with a peer in the financial industry became all about my quest. With a successful career that began at J.P. Morgan, which transitioned into helping people mitigate retirement risks, I had an excellent background in all of the traditional financial education. I began to search for methods that weren't conventional, but successful entrepreneurs had great results using. I formed a *No Stone Left Unturned* approach.

I formed masterminds and conducted interviews. I collected knowledge and experience like an addiction. I traveled the country to speak and meet people. I bought every book and course. I stayed up all night many times studying. I sat in meetings with clients when they went to see their CPA and attorney. I volunteered to help write the offering memorandum for a hedge fund. I joined financial associations. I sat for licensing exams. I got a second job in the mortgage business. I flew to different states to attend symposiums and lectures. I looked under as many stones as I could. I am became an obsessed student of finance. So, I decided to package up my experience and knowledge and provide it all in a series that I call *No Stone Left Unturned.*

The dream of finding solutions that would change my life and allow me the flexibility to spend as much time with my family as I could, drove me to find this strategy. I am so glad I did because now I can share it with you to hopefully help you to reach your goal too!

My first book shares how I was hired in 2018 to travel the country to speak to financial professionals. This book and every book after that is part of the *No Stone Left Unturned* series. I've packaged up the most powerful concepts that I've learned and applied in my own life to help you achieve financial freedom and retire successfully. My message is designed to be explained in less than 100 pages so you get the information you need quickly and take action.

While traveling the country speaking to financial professionals and working in their practices, I realized there is a large gap of knowledge in our country. It is the difference between living the life you want and struggling to make choices that aren't centered around your paycheck.

I also realized that most of the financial education we do get has the intent to sell us something. Either that or it's so boring and overly complicated that it does not engage us and, therefore, is useless. No one has ever changed their life by reading half of a book and moving on. However, when people embrace a new idea that they understand and align it with their actions, significant changes can occur and inspire them to take action to transform their lives for the better. I have made it my mission to deliver this information effectively so you can retire from the life you don't want and start living the life you do want. Thank you for reading.

The Problem: Mortgages

Worm or beetle – drought or tempest –
on a farmer's land may fall,
Each is loaded full o' ruin,
but a mortgage beats 'em all.

—Will Carleton

What are the two things people care most about when applying for a mortgage? The mortgage rate and payment amount.

What are the only metrics that should be considered for a mortgage refinance? The same thing. However, a good broker will ask about your plans to stay in the home and do a cost analysis to make sure it's worth the closing costs and fees. But is refinancing really the best thing you can do if you want to pay off your mortgage? The answer for most of us is no.

Mortgages

Banks have trained us as consumers to focus solely on the rate and payment when obtaining a mortgage, which is brilliant from the bank's perspective. What is a mortgage? Specifically, a 30-year fixed mortgage? It's a way for a bank to lock you into a contract to pay interest to them for 30 years. That's not the real definition but play along, OK?

Most people have not saved enough money to purchase a home with cash, so banks offer mortgages as an alternative. Since banks have conditioned consumers to shop for mortgages based on interest rates and payments, most consider those two factors only to determine if it is a good deal. The irony is that if your goal is to pay off the home, those are the two least contributing factors to do so. Instead, consumers should focus on time and balance.

Note: This is why you can make an extra two payments per year by switching your repayment schedule to bi-weekly payments, but more on that in the next chapter. By the way, in this book I'm not going to discuss strategies surrounding switching to a 10- or 15-year loan, making double payments, switching to bi-weekly payments, making next month's principal payment, or any other conventional method.

So, the mortgage is useful, because without its 30-year repayment amortization, most people would not be able to own a home. So, why is this a problem? If you want to pay off your home in under five years, you're stuck in this mortgage. It is not liquid; and your home is a dormant asset if you only use it to live in as your primary residence. Since equity can be gained or lost, increasing payments to pay it off faster presents risks.

But let's take a closer look at mortgages. First, look at your lending disclosure. It will tell you how much interest you will pay over the course of that 30-year mortgage. It is shocking.

Before I dive in, I'm going to use an example of an interest rate that represents an average for the last ten years. I am aware that many people are refinancing to record low interest rates of 2.5%. If you stick with me for a few more paragraphs, I will show you why this is still a mistake if your goal is to become free and clear. Remember, this book is for people who desire to own their home. If you want to mortgage your property, that is ok, just stop reading.... Now!

Let's take a look at a lending disclosure for a $300,000 purchase with a 4.25% interest rate.

Total of 360 Payments:	$531,295
Total Interest Paid:	$231,295

Wait a minute? I thought I was buying a $300,000 home, not a $531,295 home.

This is why the 30-year mortgage is pushed by the banks. They have convinced us that the 30-year is the way to go because its warm and cozy and safe. In reality, these loans make the banks a tremendous amount of money. Our nation's investment banks, local banks, and insurance companies revolve around the mortgage. It is the lifeblood of the basic investment return for these organizations, but we aren't here to talk about that. You are here to understand how to pay off your mortgage as quickly as possible.

Before we move on, there is a sector of people I need to address. They are the financial advisor or clients of the financial advisor that say: "Well, you are only paying 4.25% (or 2.5%) on your mortgage, I can make you 10%, so it doesn't make sense to pay down the mortgage." If your financial advisor has ever said this to you, after you finish this book, I want to buy my next book, "How To Find A New Financial Advisor."

"Daniel, that seems harsh. Why would you say that? It makes sense to me." Really? Well, I will tell you three reasons why you need a new financial advisor. The first two are simple.

First, they don't account for risk. When you pay off debt, you always get a return. The last time I checked, the stock market didn't come with a guarantee.

Let's say you save $12,000 per year to invest with them at 10%. That is $1,080 in interest. "Wait, I thought you said 10%, but that is only 9%!" I'm pretty sure your financial advisor doesn't volunteer their time. So, when you subtract their 1% fee, you get $1,080.

Your mortgage balance is $300,000, at 4.25%, the amount of interest you will pay in one year is $12,750. Congratulations! You made 10% and spent $11,670.

Second, it doesn't align with your goal. You want to pay off your home, not potentially grow assets and carry debt to do it. Let's look at cashflow for a moment. Let's say you owe $150,000 on your home. Your mortgage Principal, Interest, Taxes, and

Insurance (PITI) is $1,800, of which $1500 is the principal and interest. For most of us, it is our largest bill and the main barrier to retirement. If you could pay it off, that would free up $1,500 of cash flow each month. To match that, your financial advisor would have to earn $22,179.60 annually or $1,848.30 per month on that $150,000 or, as a percentage 14.785% Why so much? The 1% fee plus 22% ordinary income on the short-term gains (if that's your tax bracket and the gains are short-term). So, from a cash flow perspective, paying off your mortgage provides a way to safely create one the highest cash flows as opposed to a highly unlikely scenario of consistently earning 14.78%.

Third, let's flip this around. Say your financial advisor came to you and said, "Hey, I have this great investment. You are going to borrow $300,000 to buy a house. It will cost you $3,000-$6,000 to close on the loan. The interest rate will be 4.25%. You will slowly pay down the loan over time, gaining equity. The equity can grow by 1-2% per year, or it can be lost. That doesn't matter though, because you can't touch it for 30 years. You will pay all of the interest upfront before you actually start paying off the loan, and the total amount you will pay with interest is $531,295. You'll probably refinance the loan multiple times to get a lower rate but incur more fees and start those front-loaded interest payments all over again. Does that sound like a great idea or what?"

That conversation would never happen. Let me share with you another conversation that should never happen, but actually happens every single day. Remember the financial advisor that said, "Don't pay off your mortgage at 4.25%. I can make you 10%!" Well, what if they phrased it like this?

"Hey, you should borrow money against the equity from your home to let me invest it in the stock market for you!" How many of you just became uncomfortable reading that? It's because instinctively you know something is wrong. But that's exactly what your advisor is "advising" is in your best interest to do. That's why I said you need to fire them. By the way, any brokerage would fire an advisor who is telling clients to borrow money on the most secured debt they hold to invest in something that could lose value. Yet it happens every single day, only with a positive spin. "Don't waste money paying off 4.25% when you can earn 10%." By the way, on your balance sheet, there is no difference between taking out an equity loan to invest and investing while you have a mortgage. None. Think about that.

One last thing. I didn't write this book to replace the team you already work with. I don't want you to fire anybody. I just want you to challenge yourself to think about what you are working so hard for every day. Sometimes we put our heads down, turn off our brains, and put too much blind faith in advisors. Reevaluate and push yourself; it's healthy to assess and explore new ideas. If you arrive at the same conclusion after putting it through the stress test, then at least you can feel good knowing that you're doing your best and you're on the right path.

The strategy I'm going to show you contradicts what most banks and financial advisors do. Why? There is no money in it for them if you pay off your mortgage. Oops, I said it. Well, it's true. I didn't write this book to bash financial advisors and mortgage brokers. The truth is most people are unaware this strategy exists. When I first heard about it in 2016, I called more than 35 well-known real estate agents and loan officers in Arizona. Not one of them had heard about it. If the real estate professionals aren't in the loop, do you really expect the investment professionals to know about it?

I digress. Let's get to the solution!

The Solution: Home Equity Lines of Credit

Whatever your mind can conceive
and believe it can achieve.

– Napoleon Hill

People always ask me how is it possible to pay off a mortgage faster without making double payments? The best way I can explain it is like this: Have you ever been to the airport and seen one of those moving sidewalks? How do you get from point A to point B faster without having to run? Well, it's all about using the right tool to get the results you want more quickly.

You're paying off your mortgage by walking on the floor. I'll show you how to pay off your mortgage by getting on a moving sidewalk, and I'll equip you with roller skates and a jet pack! Ok, look, if I don't have a little bit of fun, I'm going to get bored writing, and you're going to get bored reading. It may be a book about mortgages but who said we can't have a good time. So relax, sit back, and let's get you on the

path toward financial freedom. AKA *Free and Clear.*
Oooh, that sounds great, doesn't it? Can you imagine the first time someone asks you, "How much do you owe on your home?" And you get to say, "Oh nothing. It's free and clear."

First Lien Home Equity Line of Credit

How does a first-lien home equity line of credit turn the amortization tables in your favor?

I often hear comments like the following when I discuss first-lien home equity lines of credit with others:

Home equity lines of credit make me nervous because of the variable rate.

I don't want to lose my house.

It sounds risky.

It sounds too good to be true.

I don't want a variable rate.

It took my wife six months from the time I brought this idea home before she felt comfortable with me pursuing it.

I get it. It's not taught or used often. So it must be bad, right? Let me remind you that when Henry Ford suggested a cart with no horses, people thought he was crazy. I'm not saying I am Henry Ford. I did not invent this. I also am not encouraging you to do this. I don't know your situation. My job is to educate on the subject matter. It is up to you and your team of professionals to help you with this if it's appropriate.

So, two things right off the bat. First, when I say first-lien home equity line of credit, I do not mean having your mortgage as your first loan and a home equity line of credit as a second lien like most people have. I mean refinancing your primary first-lien mortgage on to the balance of a new primary first lien home equity line of credit.

Second, most banks do not offer this product. Go figure. It was difficult for me to find a bank that did, and most of the loan officers wanted to write me a loan that was a new 30-year mortgage refinancing my current 30-year mortgage but with a lower rate.

If you go into your local bank branch and start talking about this book, there is a 90% chance that your banker will look at you like you're from Mars. At least that was my experience.

Let me explain how this works. On a regular mortgage, you have an annual percentage rate (APR), which is your interest rate, plus fees and points. A home equity line of credit uses an average daily balance meaning your payment is based on the amount of interest accrued that cycle on the balance you owe that day.

Think about your credit card. If you pay off your credit card in full each month and never carry a balance into the next cycle, do you pay interest? No! As long as you pay off the balance owed before the statement date, no interest is applied to your balance.

This is how your Home Equity Line of Credit (HELOC) will work. Of course, you won't be able to pay off the entire balance right away before the second month's statement, but remember when I said the two most important factors are always time and balance. The more you pay down the balance each month, the faster you pay off that loan. That is the secret to the entire process.

Let's recap:

1. You find a bank that can do this.

2. You find a loan officer that understands it and can write it.

3. You refinance.

How does this help you pay off your home in five years without having to make more money?

First, you have to think of your savings and mortgage as one account. Think about how smart your bank is. They pay you virtually no interest on the hard-earned money that you paid taxes on and put in a savings account at the bank. So, the bank holds the most amount of money you could save without paying you much in interest, but they are going to charge you 4.25% interest on the largest amount of money you've ever borrowed in your life.

So, why put your money in a savings account with a bank? In a standard mortgage, any extra amount paid above the minimum due is trapped in the "equity of the home," and is not liquid. Instead, you can apply your savings to the HELOC where it will remain liquid. The math does not change. Now, it's like you're earning 4.25% on that money because it is counteracting the interest rate for that portion of the HELOC balance. You are turning the amortization tables in YOUR favor. Remember: time and balance.

To go a step further, consider depositing your total net monthly income into the line, leave it there for as many days as possible each month, and then pull it out to pay all of your bills at the end of the month. That transaction will also significantly speed up your trajectory. (*This is the roller skate/jetpack combination on the moving side walk.*)

Let me elaborate. If for 25 days each month, your average daily balance is $5,000 lower because most of your net income was sitting against the line before you pull it out, that will have a huge compounding effect and dramatically assist you. Here is a simple example:

Total HELOC Balance:	$250,000
Total Net Monthly Income:	$7,000
Total Monthly Bills Excluding the HELOC Payment:	$2,000
Month One Balance:	$250,000
Payment:	$7,000
New Balance:	$243,000

Draw:	$2,000
Final Balance	$245,000
End of first year Balance:	$190,000

You're principal dropped by $60,000 in the first year!

HELOC Paid off in 50 months (Four years and two months)!

The above example is meant to show you how it works. Below is an example with the exact calculation using the same $250,000 balance and a 4.25% interest rate that increases by 1% each year.

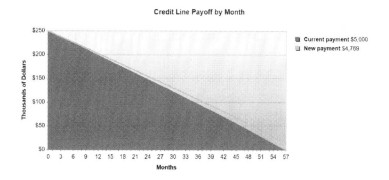

Results Summary	
Current balance	$250,000
Additional monthly charges	$0
Current monthly payment	$5000
Annual fee	$35
Interest rate (APR)	4.25%
Rate change (per year)	1%
Payoff goal (in months)	60
Draw one	$0 in 0 month(s) from now
Draw two	$0 in 0 month(s) from now
Draw three	$0 in 0 month(s) from now
Draw four	$0 in 0 month(s) from now
Payoff with a $5,000 payment	57 months
Payoff in 60 months requires	$4,768.99 per month

So, there you go! That is how you pay off your home in under five years as simple as I can make it. I wrote this book to explain this strategy better because the first few times I heard about this, it was poorly explained to me. Not fully understanding how this works delayed me in using the strategy. I do use this method myself, and I am on my way to owning my home free and clear as you read this. I want the same thing for you!

I understand that not everyone has the same scenario. If you make less or owe more, then it may take longer. You might need eight years instead of five. But that still may be better than your current trajectory, and it will help you accomplish your goal faster and save you potentially tens of thousands of dollars in interest. You need three things to use this strategy: positive monthly net income, equity in your home, and a credit score of 670+. You might be able to get one with a fair score of at least 640, but it depends on other factors, such as your debt-to-income ratio and reserves, just like qualifying for a regular mortgage.

Three Downsides to the HELOC

1. Your payment may increase each month if you pay only the minimum. However, if you follow this method, that shouldn't be a problem.

2. It has a variable rate. While writing this, and while that is not directly tied to consumer HELOC rates, we also have the largest national debt that we've ever had. What is the incentive for the Government to raise rates? When I calculated my HELOC, I used an interest rate of 4% and increased it by 2% each year. So, by the time I was free and clear, my loan was at a 14% interest rate, and it illustrated that I was still able to pay it off in 41 months because the balance decreased so much it did not matter.

3. Higher interest rates and closing costs. Let's not step over dollars to pick up pennies. The goal is to pay off your home. It's not too good to be true. It is, however, too good to be free.

Warning: Compound interest can work *for* you and *against* you. If you do not follow the steps correctly, you will have the opposite result, and the variable rate and average daily balance will quickly work against you. This strategy is only for someone who can appropriately manage debt and is very financially disciplined.

There is one other strategy to accelerate your pay off date using a second HELOC. You mostly do the same thing, but it involves using a credit card as well. I'm not going to write about it in detail, although the people that support it swear it is the best way to do this. When you start researching this strategy online, you will find that these two camps are extremely divided, and this often results in another void into which the potential consumer falls.

At least that's what happened to me. I tried it first myself and found it has a slower result. It's like stepping onto that walking sidewalk and being trapped behind someone who won't walk (I know, I know. It's a pet peeve of mine as well). It creates doubt and causes you to pause. The strategy does work, and it is even a little less risky by my analysis – it's just not as quick. I feel that it is less risky in the sense that if you are not that financially disciplined, it presents less of a chance that you will not stick to the process. Since it involves using a supplemental line of credit on a portion of your equity, your potential variable rate and increased payments are limited. If you want to be free and clear in four to eight years, then the strategy I described will bring the fastest result.

It's really that simple. There is no reason to over complicate it. If you are motivated to pay down your debts aggressively, then follow these steps:

Step 1. Decide if this is the house you intend to remain in once you pay off your mortgage.

Step 2. Honestly evaluate if you are financially disciplined to deposit your net income and only pull out what you need. This transaction is mandatory for the best results.

Step 3. Do you have your ingredients? Positive monthly net income, equity in your home, and a fair to good credit score 640+?

Step 4. Run the calculation. Find a mortgage broker that can review your scenario to test this process. You can even factor in other debts that can be rolled into your refinance like a car loan or credit card debt. This may present more cashflow and allow you to pay those debts down faster as well. If you have six to 12 months of reserves in savings, see what impact it has to include that in the line, since it offers liquidity. See if your new pay back schedule makes sense. Warning: Always speak to your advisor before refinancing unsecured debt into your mortgage. Every state has different creditor laws, and you want to make sure that you are aware of the potential issues in trading your unsecured debt with arguably your most secured debt.

Step 5. Take action! If you decide after careful examination and working with your team of advisors that this is right for you, then be proactive and take initiative. Remember, no one is going to do it for you. It is up to you to take control of your financial future and make it happen.

This strategy has changed my life and my trajectory towards financial freedom. Clients and friends thank me all of the time for what this strategy has done for their lives as well. I hope that it can bring value to you on your journey. As always thank you for reading and take care.

If you would like to further discuss the strategies in this book, I am offering a one-time 15-minute Zoom call to anyone who purchases my book and leaves me a review. To schedule a call with me, the author, or a member of my team, please visit:

www.DanielRondberg.com

Resources

Listed below are two companies that can provide further education on these strategies. I do not endorse or directly recommend that you use either of these companies:

First-Lien HELOC

Replace Your Mortgage
www.ReplaceYourMortgage.com
(615) 925-3887

Second-Lien HELOC

The Speed Equity Mortgage Acceleration System
www.SpeedEquity.com/WP
(206) 774-3673

Watch a video explanation here:
www.RetirementSimplified.org/30yearto5

About the Author

Daniel Rondberg
The Retirement Specialist

Daniel Rondberg
Nation's First Financial
Retirement Specialist

The Retirement Research Foundation
Course Educator

Danny@dannyrondberg.com

Daniel Rondberg is a retirement authority. He's taught financial professionals and consumers all over the country. His mission is simple: reach as many pre-retirees as soon as possible to help them enjoy the best years of their lives!

Daniel Rondberg began his career working at JP Morgan, but later felt drawn to embrace the family business and went on to become an independent retirement specialist at Nation's First Financial in their Mesa, Arizona office. Daniel's success has been quick and consistent. The value he provides is demonstrated to his clients through his focus on tax reduction and retirement security, although his greatest strength is listening and honoring his clients' concerns by customizing solutions that align with their core beliefs.

In addition, he teaches educational workshops on retirement and is a published author in a well-known industry trade publication furnished by Ideal Producers Group. In 2016, 2017, 2018, and 2019, he was recognized as the number one life specialist by the same company.

He has gone on to become an international best-selling author with both of his first two books:

No Stone Left Unturned (How To Cash In On This Hidden Treasure In The Tax code)
https://amzn.to/3gYTtCb

Retirement Simplified (The Two Step Formula to Retire Wealthy and Worry-Free).
https://amzn.to/2DUe1gJ

Daniel enjoys helping people breathe easy when it comes to retirement and traveling with his family. He lives in Mesa, Arizona with his lovely wife, Jennifer, and his daughters Cassidy and Spencer. Together, they are dedicated to traveling the world and sharing their message.

In addition to be an educator and speaker, Daniel is a published author and creator of the Life Hacks Unlimited Life Program. He manages a team that oversees more than $100 million in retirement assets and life insurance benefits for his clients.

Contact Daniel

My personal site:
www.DanielRondberg.com

My Vlog:
www.RetirementByDanielRondberg.com

My FREE Social Security Maximization Webinar:
www.RetirementResearchFoundation.org/Social-Security-Maximization-Webinar

My Agency's site:
www.NationsFirstFin.com

My Industry Insider's podcast:
https://RealWealthMedia.com/Danny-Rondberg

My YouTube Channel:
www.YouTube.com/channel/
UC52cim- 6wfLu7WQnlyJtfUxQ

My Podcast:
www.BuzzSprout.com/695890

Sources

https://thinksaveretire.com/think-you-need-a-2000-sqft-house-to-be-comfortable-think-again/

www.InspirationalStories.com/quotes/t/about-mortgage/

www.Amortization-Calc.com/mortgage-calculator/

www.BankRate.com/calculators/home-equity/line-of-credit-debt-payoff-calculator.aspx

Made in the USA
Middletown, DE
09 December 2020

26897934R00033